for parents only

discussion guide

helping you get inside
the head of your kid

shaunti feldhahn
lisa a. rice

MULTNOMAH
BOOKS

D0106624

FOR PARENTS ONLY DISCUSSION GUIDE
PUBLISHED BY MULTNOMAH BOOKS
12265 Oracle Boulevard, Suite 200
Colorado Springs, Colorado 80921
A division of Random House Inc.

Scripture quotations are taken from The Holy Bible, English Standard Version, copyright © 2001 by Crossway Bibles, a division of Good News Publishers. Used by permission. All rights reserved.

ISBN 978-1-59052-990-4

Printed in the United States of America
2007—First Edition

10 9 8 7 6 5 4 3 2 1

Contents

One

LOOKING IN
ON GROWING UP

*Taking a tour inside your
kid's head and heart*

I f your experience is anything like ours, we imagine you've found parenting to be a dizzying combination of joy, frustration, amazement, confusion, delight, and anxiety—sometimes all within a single hour. It's both exciting and sobering to watch as those little fat babies who coo and smile delightedly at us transform into long-legged teenagers who shake their heads over our complete lack of coolness.

It feels like one day we're pushing them on the swings and the next we're pushing them into college. And that seeming nanosecond of time between the two is, obviously, the most formative period of our children's lives. As we help our kids navigate these foundational years, most of us realize we need a little guidance ourselves.

As we embarked on several research projects to help people understand those closest to them, the two of us realized that unraveling the mystery of what's going on inside our sons and daughters was one of the most important things we could ever do. So after a year of intensive research, focus groups, and surveys of kids and teens across the country, we revealed our findings in the book *For Parents Only.*

Understanding Our Kids

There's an ancient Hebrew proverb that says, "Happy the generation where the great listen to the small, for it follows that in such a generation the small will listen to the great." It is for this reason we're relaying to you what our children are privately thinking and feeling, even though we certainly do not endorse all of it. But we believe listening to these heart cries is a critical step in building the relationship that will allow your kids to listen to you and your guidance for years to come.

The chart below offers a summary of the six key insights we uncovered about the inner lives of kids—the things they say too many parents "just don't get." The left column outlines what we often *assume* about our kids based on their behavior when they hit the 'tween and teen years, while the right column reveals the surprises about what's really going inside their minds and hearts.

When They Hit the Teen Years	
Here's What We Think Is Happening	Here's What's Really Happening
Peer pressure pushes kids to rebel and behave in reckless ways without thinking through the consequences.	The intoxicating nature of freedom—and the fear of losing it—can lead even good kids to make choices that look like recklessness and rebellion, but directly addressing their craving for independence will help them build responsibility.

Teens seem to reject parents and their values, no longer caring much what their parents think.	Separating themselves from their parents' identity is one of the only ways healthy teenagers can develop their own; but even as they seem to push us away, our children still secretly want to know our values and need our affirmation of who they are becoming.
Teens don't want rules or discipline.	Although our teens test our authority and argue with rules, they secretly want us to stand firm as parents and will lose respect for us if we don't.
When kids make mistakes, they disregard their parents' opinions or criticism.	Although they may not look like it, kids want the security of knowing we are making the effort to understand them and will be there for them regardless of their mistakes—but kids will emotionally shut out a parent they see as judgmental.
Kids say parents don't listen.	Kids tend to stop talking because they perceive parents as rotten listeners but will open up when we prove we're safe and calmly acknowledge their feelings before addressing a problem.
Teens give in easily to negative attitudes—afflicting their families with sullenness, anger, or back talk—over what seem to be minor issues.	What looks like an attitude problem may actually be a sign of insecurity, but actively countering our children's fears can build their confidence and help them become more respectful of parents and others.

As we travel and speak to various groups about these and other findings, we frequently hear, "How can I apply these truths to *my* life, with *my* kids?"

This discussion guide will help you do just that. It's designed to be used in two different ways: (1) as a catalyst for group discussion and life application with other parents, and (2) as a helpful road map for initiating some eye-opening conversations with your child.

Each chapter in this guide corresponds to a chapter subject in the main book:

- Chapter 2: Freedom
- Chapter 3: Identity
- Chapter 4: Taking Charge
- Chapter 5: Security
- Chapter 6: Listening
- Chapter 7: Attitude
- Chapter 8: How Your Kid Really Feels About You

For consistency and ease of use, each chapter follows the same format, opening with tools for group discussion and personal reflection, then highlighting practical ways to test and apply your insights in your daily interaction with your child.

Each chapter has basically the same layout. Among other features you'll find:

- a Recap of key insights from the book
- Key Questions for discussion and/or personal reflection

- Life Story case studies with follow-up questions for practice in getting inside your kid's head (in other words, learning the skill of reading their minds)
- a Kid Perspective and a Parent Response—a new quote that reflects what a real-life teen is thinking about the topic at hand, and an opportunity for you to respond to that input
- Weekly Challenges—action items to help you practice your new insights during the week

And also...

- Bringing It Home—standalone sections (that parents can use even without a group) to help you connect with your child on each topic and hear what he or she has to say

Because every discussion group has its own character and goals, and each individual parent has different primary concerns, this guide is designed to be flexible. You can use it over any number of weeks, mixing and matching the different elements in whatever way best suits your needs.

For example, your group may opt to cover only a single subject over one or two sessions, trying to hit as many of the different features as time allows. Alternatively, you may want to combine chapters and only tackle the Key Questions in each. Your group may even want to skip most of the Key Questions and focus your time on the case studies and Weekly Challenges. We encourage you to pick and choose the combination that works best for you.

We also hope the Bringing It Home sections will help you talk to your child about these subjects—to hear his or her thoughts, fears, and desires directly. (Please see page 14 for more explanation.)

Though our findings primarily focus on the teen and preteen years, you can also adapt the questions for younger kids, to lay a solid foundation of understanding before adolescence arrives. (For example, you might re-phrase a question such as, "How can you address this problem this week?" to ask, "What can you do that might prevent this problem down the road?")

As parents ourselves, we know that it's not always easy to really hear what the kids are saying. But as we interacted with all these amazing young people during our research, we gathered some terrific nuggets of wisdom about how to apply their insights to our parenting. We hope that you, too, will find fresh insight from this eye-opening journey inside your kid's head and heart.

Best to you in your journey,

Shaunti & Lisa

P.S. If your group has an introductory week, here's your first Weekly Challenge question:

> **Weekly Challenge:** This week, look at the chart on pages 2–3 and identify which revelation you already have best incorporated into your parent-ing approach—and which is the most likely to require changes in your life.

Two

REBEL WITH A CAUSE

Why even good kids go crazy for freedom, and how to restore sanity

Weekly Challenge Report: Which of the six key insights are you already effectively addressing as a parent? Which do you think will require the most change from you?

Recap

Much of the behavior that parents attribute to rebellion or peer pressure actually is motivated by a child's addictive quest for *freedom*. To a teen, freedom is like an intoxicating drug, and "under the influence" of freedom, kids may do stupid things, not thinking about the consequences. Kids deeply fear having their freedom taken away, and in order to get freedom and avoid losing it, they may even lie and hide things from parents. But, ironically, too much freedom can be scary, and your child actually wants your guidance in managing his growing independence.

"Freedom is cocaine to a teenager. It's intoxicating. It's addictive. And it is often their biggest motivator. They will do anything to get it, and they are terrified of losing it." —Dr. Julie Carbery, as quoted in FPO, p. 15

"An enraged teenager's out-of-proportion response to your words or actions may be a sign that you've set off her ultrasensitive 'loss of freedom' radar." —FPO, p. 25

Key Questions

1. What revelation from this chapter did you find most challenging?

2. When kids make questionable choices, does it *matter* whether those choices are driven by a craving for freedom rather than by rebellion or peer pressure? In cases where freedom *is* the underlying motivation, should that affect your parenting in any way?

3. What specific freedoms do you think most motivate your child? Which might he most fear losing?

4. What signals does your child send when her spirit is clamoring for freedom? What does she say and do that indicates a strong internal want?

5. What is your child's typical response to any discipline that affects his freedoms?

6. What area is the biggest source of conflict in your home regarding your rules versus your child's freedom? What new ideas did you gain from this chapter for potentially reducing that conflict?

7. Describe an occasion when you chalked up your child's behavior to a heart issue, such as rebellion, when in fact it might have sprung from this quest for freedom. If you can, also give an example of when you correctly sensed your child's driving hunger for freedom. How did your response differ in each case, and how did your approach affect your child's attitude toward you?

8. Consider this passage from the letter the apostle Paul wrote to the church at Ephesus (Ephesians 6:4): "Fathers, do not provoke your children to anger, but bring them up in the discipline and instruction of the Lord." How does this apply to a parent's relationship with a freedom-intoxicated kid?

Life Story

Julia burst into her parents' bedroom and flung her-self on the bed. "Mom, please!" She had tears in her eyes. "Please let me go to the party at Joey's house tonight."

Her mother raised an eyebrow. "You know you're grounded from parties, honey. Until you get back to a B average in biology. And you'll have to get As on the next two tests to do that..."

"But I *did* get an A on last Friday's test, and there's not another test for two weeks! You guys are so unfair," Julia wailed. "Okay, I admit it: I was stupid not to study and fail that biology test, but I've learned my lesson. You grounded me from my cell phone *and* MySpace *and* hanging out with my friends just because of one bad grade! Mom, I *have* to go to Joey's house tonight. It's the only time he's actually *invited* me to anything. And because you took away my cell phone, I've already missed a bunch of text messages, and I have no idea what is going on, and people think I'm totally out of it, and they're going to stop inviting me to things alto-gether. Please, Mom! Can't you remember how hard it is to be my age?"

Case Study Questions

1. Drawing on your study of this chapter, what deep-rooted fear did her parents' punishment trigger in Julia?

2. To help you put yourself in Julia's shoes, let's relate her situation to something in your world. How would you feel if your phone or Internet access was suddenly cut off and you couldn't get any answers about when it would resume? To help you really feel Julia's pain, suppose your employer had been paying the bill for your phone and Internet but cut it off after a bad work review. What thoughts and feelings would you have when you first learned of the decision—and then during the days when you had no service? How might your feelings compare to Julia's?

3. Stay in Julia's shoes and project your fears forward to the near and far future. What scenarios might be playing in her mind about what could happen as a result of her loss of connection to the social scene? How does she feel about this?

4. If Julia's parents view her as a rational teen who knows that there are consequences for breaking rules, how might they involve her in the discipline process? What alternative punishment might Julia suggest that would avoid triggering the fear identified in question 1? What are the potential drawbacks and benefits of giving her a say in this?

5. Was Julia's tirade appropriate or justified? Why or why not? If you have seen such emotion-filled tirades in your home, what is your typical response? What can you do, moving forward, to assuage the strong emotion and underlying fears?

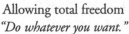 **Kid Perspective:** "Parents can be so inflexible at times and so married to their rules. I feel like I get overpunished for the smallest offenses and even for things I sometimes can't help. If they're gonna think we're rebellious and horrible, we'll just become that way—even though it wasn't our intention! We'll just give up trying after a while if they ground us from everything for the tiniest reasons. We're not perfect; we just want to be trusted to try some things and fail sometimes without the hammer coming down."

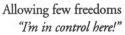 **Parent Response:** Do you think your child may perceive that the "hammer comes down" for even small offenses? Or might he (secretly) think the opposite—that he has too many unchecked freedoms? On the following freedom scale, where do you think your parenting falls? If you had to guess, where would your *child* say that your parenting falls?

| 1 | 2 | 3 | 4 | 5 | 6 | 7 | 8 | 9 | 10 |

Allowing total freedom   Allowing few freedoms
"Do whatever you want."   *"I'm in control here!"*

Weekly Challenge: (1) Observe the kids in your life—including your child's friends—and try to spot three situations where they may be feeling their freedom is stifled. Take note of the signals you observe. (2) If a discipline or punishment is necessary this week, look for an option that (if appropriate) could avoid triggering your child's specific loss-of-freedom fear.

Someone Once Said...

"Teenagers are people who act like babies if they're not treated like adults." —*MAD* magazine

To keep in mind: In each chapter you'll find this Bringing It Home section, which supplies some ideas for discussing these topics with your kids. But we also believe the *way* you discuss them is important. You may want to casually set the stage for these conversations by commenting, perhaps as your child heads off to do homework, that you really want to understand him better and are doing some homework yourself on how teenagers think.

As we note in the book, our skittish little deer can be easily scared off by too much pressure or intensity, so we encourage you to watch for the right opportunity and time to have these conversations, perhaps plying your child with a snack when he comes home from school, driving with him in the car, or late at night giving him your full attention before he goes to sleep.

We've provided quite a few conversation-starter questions on each topic, so we also suggest you look through them ahead of time to see which ones might be most helpful for you and easiest for your child to discuss. You'll also find questions related to our national survey to help you figure out how your child's responses compare—though we've tried to rephrase them in ways that will both help your child feel at ease and lead you to a deeper understanding of how he or she thinks.

Obviously, your kid may be reluctant to share his true feelings about certain things, and that's okay. But if you determine to approach things calmly, no matter what he tells you, we believe communication will flow more freely as you explain (and show) that you want to hear what he really thinks and feels.

BRINGING IT HOME: CONVERSATIONS WITH YOUR CHILD ON FREEDOM

Hey, Kids...

- As I learn more about what is often going on inside teenagers, I realize I may have misunderstood some of your actions and thought you were being rebellious, when in reality you might not have wanted to be rebellious but were acting out of a longing for freedom. For example, when you did/said this _____, I thought it was because of _____. Now I realize maybe you were really doing/saying this: _____; is that correct? Can you give me more examples?
- Do you ever feel that I'm not respecting your need for freedom? Can you give me an example? What can I do or say differently to show that I want to guide your quest for freedom in a healthy way?
- Which of the freedoms that you have now are the most important to you? What freedoms do you most look forward to gaining in the months and years ahead?

- What does it feel like to you when I take away a given freedom as punishment? If you had the option, what punishments or consequences would you choose that wouldn't make you feel like your most important freedoms are being stifled?

Optional: How would your child answer the survey?
- When you feel strongly about doing something I'd normally say no to, are you generally motivated by a feeling of rebellion, peer pressure, a desire to do what *you* want (freedom), or something else?
- Are you ever tempted to hide information from me because you're worried about how I will react? What's an example of a time that my reaction might have seemed like overkill to you?

The BIG Idea

The one main idea I'm taking away from this week's discussion is…

_____

_____

_____

_____

_____

_____

_____

Three

WHO *ARE* YOU?

*Why your child suddenly treats you
like an alien—and acts like one too*

> Weekly Challenge Report: Did you spot kids who
> may have felt stifled in their freedoms? What did
> that look like? Did you find an opportunity to try
> a different discipline approach to avoid triggering
> your child's fear of losing a specific freedom?

Recap

In order to become well-adjusted adults, our children *must* develop their own identity. Parents tend to know this, but we may not realize that one of the only ways they can do that is to question and even reject—at least for a time—the only identity they've ever known, which is ours. The good news is that kids want a strong sense of family heritage and values to which they can return. As your child pulls away in sometimes hurtful ways, she needs you to guide rather than prevent her search for identity—and she longs for your affirmation of the person she is becoming.

"We often don't realize that when our children seem embarrassed by us, are hostile toward us, or—most worrisome—begin to question the values that they've been taught their whole lives, it is usually directly related to a search for themselves." —FPO, p. 42

"The only way he can build his own castle is to dismantle what you and other influencers have built and to restructure those materials into something all his own." —FPO, p. 46

"When your kid declares, 'You just don't understand me!' what he's really saying is, 'I'm changing so much that I don't even understand myself, and it's scary. So I know that there's no way that someone else can possibly keep up.'" —older teen quoted in FPO, p. 55

Key Questions

1. What in this chapter surprised you most?

2. Do you agree that kids should be allowed to pursue their own identity, apart from their parents? Why or why not?

3. Describe a few examples you've seen of confusing comments or behaviors that make a lot more sense in light of a kid's search for identity.

4. If you can, describe a time when you might have made your child feel that she had to be an extension of you, rather than letting her pull away and figure out her own identity. Do you think your action made the area of concern better or worse? Next time you encounter a similar situation, what might you do differently?

5. What steps can you take to create a safe place for your child to "build his own castle"?

6. What are some signs of your child's evolving definition of self (in a MySpace description, room decorations, entertainment choices, etc.)? How do you feel about her emerging identity as

it differs from how you've always known her? As you wrestle through your internal feelings, how can you best ensure that your external reaction (to her) is productive?

7. What can you do to show your interest in the person your child is becoming? If you've done that already at times, what has been his response?

8. What are the core truths or values you hope your child will carry with her when she starts her own family? In what ways are you living out those beliefs and values in your family for her to see?

Life Story

Thomas's family had always been active churchgoers. They attended services most Sundays and often got involved in other functions during the week. For Thomas, that included youth group meetings and events on Friday nights, when the high-schoolers met up for everything from regular Bible studies to bowling tournaments at the local mall.

But during the past few months, Thomas's parents had grown worried. More and more, he resisted going to church with them on Sunday morning. He sometimes grumbled about the Friday night youth meetings, but was generally willing to go if at least a few of his buddies planned to be there. Sunday services, however, were increasingly a different story.

Thomas's dad, Jack, had to put his foot down several times, telling his son things like, "In this family, we worship God together. It's important that you get this foundation, and if you don't get in the car right now, that's the end of playing football this fall."

During one Sunday-morning confrontation, Thomas protested, "This is crazy! No one else in my *whole school* goes to church every Sunday. I'm like the only guy I know whose parents force him to go. It's boring and I've heard it all for years. I won't get anything out of it anyway, so why should I waste my time?"

Case Study Questions

1. What do you think is the main reason Thomas's parents have required him to attend church? What concern is at the root of their strong stance on this issue?

2. Now, put yourself in Thomas's shoes—if you can stand the thought of the size 12 sneakers he wore to play hoops with the guys last night! Drawing on what you learned in this chapter, what internal factor or pressure is likely driving his external resistance to attending church?

3. Stay in Thomas's shoes. As his parents demonstrate their determination to enforce this family ideal, is that internal pressure relieved or exacerbated?

4. You're still looking at the world through Thomas's eyes. Does he understand his parents' underlying concern, as discussed in question 1? If yes, how does that compare to his *own* concern? If no, what does that suggest about how his parents should approach this issue?

5. Have you seen this type of situation played out when parents—you or someone you know—want to instill specific beliefs, values, or priorities in a child? What are the two extreme, opposite ways that parents might deal with a teen's resistance? What are the ramifications of each for the relationship between parents and kid? for the child's perspective regarding the value at issue?

6. Based on what you learned in this chapter, how would you advise Thomas's parents to approach this issue going forward?

What strategy could they adopt to acknowledge their son's inner realities without giving up on something that they believe will have lasting consequences?

7. What other options could his parents pursue to accomplish their underlying goal?

Kid Perspective: "Kids need to experience things on their own. Parents can't force kids to do things. They can tell kids stuff, but we want to make our own choices and not feel we're being held back. We want to be different from our parents…to try something new. Even if our parents are good and we love them, we want to be ourselves and to live our own lives."

Parent Response: Why might you find it difficult to let your kids experience things on their own? Can you *ever* be such a great parent that your kids would want to be exactly like you? What might be some positive results of allowing your child to forge a fresh path, separate from yours?

Weekly Challenge: (1) Observe the kids in your life and try to spot examples of how their words or actions might be attempts to answer the question "Who am I?" (2) If you find yourself at odds with your child in a noncrucial situation, take a deep breath and experiment with *not* pressing your opinions, values, or tastes, and instead allowing your child the space to "build her own castle." Take note of how she responds to this alternate tactic.

Someone Once Said...

"Some authority on parenting once said, 'Hold them very close and then let them go.' This is the hardest truth for a father to learn: that his children are continuously growing up and moving away from him (until, of course, they move back in)." —Bill Cosby

"Adolescence is a period of rapid changes. Between the ages of twelve and seventeen, for example, a parent ages as much as twenty years." —Al Bernstein

BRINGING IT HOME: CONVERSATIONS WITH YOUR CHILD ON IDENTITY

Hey, Kids...

- Some teenagers feel that their parents don't understand them, and certainly you've gone through a lot of changes. Are there any areas in which you feel I haven't quite kept up? Can you give me an example of a time when you think I treated you like the kid you used to be rather than the person you are now?

- Can you describe a time you felt I didn't understand something about you and wasn't getting what you were trying to tell me? What about a time I did understand and got it right, in your eyes?

- If I were meeting you for the first time, what are the top three things you'd want me to know about the person you are? What interests and skills, dreams and goals do you think best define who you are or who you want to become?

- Do you feel free to be yourself in this family? Do we ever make you uncomfortable about showing who you really are? Can you give me some examples? What can we do to help you feel free to express who you are?

- As we learn, will you help us to understand you by *gently* pointing out when we do or say something that makes you feel stifled in your search for your own identity?

Optional: How would your child answer the survey?

- How would you describe our family's top priorities, values, and beliefs to someone else? Which of those values, if any, will you want to pass on to your own kids someday? Which are you still not sure about?

The BIG Idea

The one main idea I'm taking away from this week's discussion is...

_____

_____

_____

_____

Four

THE GOOD THING ABOUT BEING THE BAD GUY

Why your child secretly hopes you'll stand your ground

Weekly Challenge Report: Did you spot a time when a child's words or actions hinted at the internal question "Who am I?" How successful were you at resisting the temptation to impose your own opinion, and how did your child respond?

Recap

While your child will likely object to your authority, she really does want you to act like a parent rather than a friend. On our survey, three out of four kids confessed that they want parents who set reasonable rules, ensure they do their homework, care about whom they hang out with, try to create family time, and stay involved in their lives. By contrast, they lose respect for parents who let things slide or don't enforce the rules. Even "good kids" need watchful attention and discipline. As long as your child knows you aren't just "showing who's boss" but actively trying to help her develop responsibility, she will (secretly) feel loved and cared for when you take charge.

"Love makes decisions in the best interest of the kid, no matter how much the kid kicks and screams." —high-school sophomore quoted in FPO, *p. 72*

"As kids explained their respect for parents who take charge, there was one clear caveat: parents have to be willing to explain why *the rules and boundaries exist and not appear arbitrary, so the teens can understand the reasons for themselves."* —FPO, *p. 79*

"Literally hundreds of teens…said they might resist their parents' rules now but will probably want to parent their own children in exactly the same way." —FPO, *p. 86*

Key Questions

1. What in this chapter did you find most surprising? most encouraging?

2. If you can, describe a time when your child complained about your setting firm boundaries but probably later appreciated it, whether openly or secretly.

3. What do you think prompts some parents to act more like their kids' friend than a parent? What results have you observed—in your own family or in those you know—when this happens?

4. How can you balance your child's need for you to take charge with his desire for freedom? What steps can you take to demonstrate you're taking charge in order to help her become responsible, not just for the sake of showing who's the boss?

5. List some examples of how you check up on your child's various activities, including online interactions.

6. On the following flexibility scale, where do you think you fall? And if you had to guess, where would your *child* say that you fall?

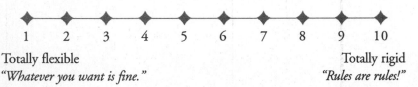

1   2   3   4   5   6   7   8   9   10

Totally flexible   Totally rigid
"Whatever you want is fine."   *"Rules are rules!"*

7. What are some techniques you might use to both remain calm when confronted with disobedience and avoid knee-jerk solutions in favor of ones that have been thought through?

8. Considering all the areas of concern that can arise in the life of a teenager, how can you as a parent distinguish between the areas in which you *must* remain firm and the areas in which you could allow your child to test her own judgment as part of the maturing process?

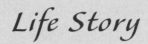

Life Story

Ever since middle school Tessa's parents had worried about her shy streak and difficulty making friends, so they were delighted when their daughter finally found a group of friends who accepted her. They hadn't actually met many of these kids, except for five minutes now and then when Tessa's mom picked her up after school. But they hadn't heard anything bad about them either, and were relieved at their daughter's new self-confidence.

But as the months went by, Tessa's parents found themselves feeling a bit uneasy, especially once Tessa got her driver's license and began driving herself to and from school and elsewhere. She was always out at some activity or over at a friend's house—"just hanging out"— and sometimes they felt like they hardly saw her for whole days in a row, except late at night and early in the morning when she was driving away to school.

Tessa's parents encouraged her to invite her friends over, but she wasn't interested. She'd also begun to miss curfew—the movie was running late or it took longer than expected to drive a friend home. And twice, Tessa's mom had found empty beer cans when she cleaned out Tessa's car. When her parents asked about it, Tessa apologized for letting her friends drink in the car, assuring them she hadn't joined in. And she began to get upset when they questioned her a bit more, accusing them of not trusting her.

Her parents also worried about her grades. Each time they saw a C or a D on a test, they talked to her about it and she promised to work harder, but nothing really changed. They tried grounding her from driving, but neither of them could afford the time to drive her to all her activities, so it was more hassle than it was worth. Frustrated, Tessa's parents consoled themselves with the thought that everyone goes through this with teenagers and that it was bound to get better soon.

Case Study Questions

1. Given how they're responding to her behavior, what seems to be the highest concern Tessa's parents have for their daughter?

2. Put yourself in Tessa's shoes. She lives at home but often goes for days without seeing much of her parents, now that she's driving herself to school and other activities. What might be her impression of how they feel about her?

3. Stay in Tessa's shoes. She's enjoying the acceptance of her new friends and is glad that her parents didn't flip out too much when they found the beer cans. Her friends' drinking and other

risky behaviors make her uneasy at times, but she doesn't really have an excuse *not* to participate. At those times, what might she feel about her parents and their approach?

4. Looking at things through Tessa's eyes, how does she feel about her parents and the fact that they aren't setting firm boundaries or enforcing the ones they try? Does she appreciate and love them more? What might the fact that she didn't bother to conceal the beer cans reveal about her opinion of her parents?

5. How might Tessa view her parents in ten years if this trend continues?

6. What could these parents have done differently? Going forward, list some actions her parents could take, both now and in the weeks to come. How might Tessa respond to those actions in the short term? long term?

Kid Perspective: "Jenny's mom babies her so much that she's become useless in some areas. Her mom has shielded her from all responsibility, so we can't rely on her to hold up her end of the deal at school with projects and stuff. And she has no boundaries with guys or friendships because she's never had any at home. The rest of us see this and are grateful for our parents who love us enough to be unpopular at times."

Parent Response: How willing are you to be unpopular with your kid and/or her friends? What are some areas where you may have undermined your child's sense of responsibility by shielding her from the consequences of her actions? What value do you place on having your child's approval? Why? What if you didn't have it?

Weekly Challenge: (1) Track the times you have a conflict with your child because you held to a rule or expectation—or *would* have had a conflict if you had really enforced it. (2) Based on what happens in the hours and days after each incident, assess whether you've found the right balance between enforcing the rule and letting it go.

Someone Once Said...

"I think of discipline as the continual everyday process of helping a child learn self-discipline." —Fred Rogers

"If you have never been hated by your child, you have never been a parent." —Bette Davis

"Parents who are afraid to put their foot down usually have children who step on their toes." —Chinese proverb

BRINGING IT HOME:
CONVERSATIONS WITH YOUR
CHILD ON TAKING CHARGE

Hey, Kids...

- Where would you say my parenting falls on the following scale?

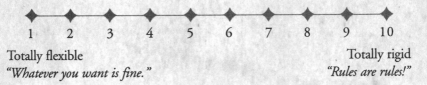

| 1 | 2 | 3 | 4 | 5 | 6 | 7 | 8 | 9 | 10 |

Totally flexible   Totally rigid
"Whatever you want is fine."   *"Rules are rules!"*

- I need to be the one in charge, in order to help you learn how to responsibly take charge of your own life. To do this in the way *you* need, it would be helpful to hear your honest perspective in a few areas. Thinking back over the past few months or years:

  a. Was there a time you resented my holding to a rule or expectation but later were secretly glad?

  b. How about a time when I held firm and you still think I was wrong for doing so?

  c. How about the reverse? Was there a time that I didn't hold you to a rule (or didn't have a rule to begin with) and later you wished I had?

  d. Have I ever been flexible and let something go, and you still agree that that was totally the right decision?

- When you look at how your friends interact with their parents, are there some things you'd like to see me do differently when it comes to setting or enforcing rules? What are some things you've seen that make you wonder if the parents really have their kids' best interests at heart?

- I'd like to work through some critical-thinking skills to help you make wise decisions. Think about "a gray area" activity— something that might be questionable, not clearly right or wrong. Perhaps even something I might recently have said "no" to. Let's test the activity as you ask yourself these questions:

  a. Does this activity or friend help me or hinder me from reaching my God-given purposes in life?

  b. Is this activity a mark of being someone who goes along with the crowd, or a mark of being set apart and willing to stand alone for what I believe?

  c. Does this activity have the potential of trapping me and drawing me into more unwise choices?

  d. What does my conscience say?

  Have these questions changed your mind about this subject at all? Why or why not?

- What are some areas where you're happy with our current boundaries? In what areas could I help you feel safer by getting a little more involved and setting a few more limits? Where would you like to see me back off while still helping you think through decisions on your own?

- Would it be helpful if we updated our discipline strategy and brought you in on the process? What are some areas where you'd like to set some rules and boundaries for yourself *that we could agree with,* along with appropriate consequences for breaking them?

The BIG Idea

The one main idea I'm taking away from this week's discussion is...

Five

I WILL BE HERE FOR YOU

How to help teens feel secure in the ascent to adulthood, even when they lose their footing

Weekly Challenge Report: As you weathered conflict or eluded potential clashes this week, what percentage of time did you enforce versus let it go? Looking back at the results of each, do you think you got it right each time? What, if anything, might you do differently next time?

Recap

As discussed in the previous chapter, kids need us to take charge—but they need us to do so in a very specific way. Kids say they feel more secure when their parents also make the effort to understand them and be part of their world. When they make mistakes, even though those mistakes might have external consequences, our kids want to know that we'll be there for them through it all and will handle those mistakes calmly. But if kids feel we are being judgmental or overreacting, they'll shut us out emotionally. As in Jesus's parable of the prodigal son, your child needs you to demonstrate that your love is unconditional, pursuing, and forgiving.

"I wish I could really know that, no matter what stupid thing I did, my parents would be there to hear me out and support me." —teenager quoted in FPO, p. 104

"As many kids pointed out, how can your child be assured that you'll 'be there' for him if you don't even know him? The key, they said, is demonstrating that you want to know and understand him." —FPO, p. 95

"Just as we need those close to us to offer grace when we make mistakes, our kids need us to recognize that they will blow it once in a while. As one teen put it: 'The sooner that parents realize kids will make mistakes and meet them in the middle, the better.' " —FPO, p. 108

Key Questions

1. What challenged you most in this chapter?

2. Think of a recent occasion when you reacted to your child in a way she might have perceived as judgmental. What underlying concern prompted you to react this way? What was your child's response? In hindsight, would you change anything?

3. Describe a time when your child suffered the consequences of a poor choice from someone other than you, but also saw that you were going to clearly love and support him throughout the situation. What was the outcome?

4. What is one way you're making an effort to be a part of your child's world? What other opportunities could you take to show that you're interested in the day-to-day stuff of life?

5. How can you tell when your child is shutting you out emotionally? What might she say or do to signal that she's feeling insecure in your relationship?

6. Read the story of the prodigal son (Luke 15:11–24). How might you have reacted if the returning prodigal were your son?

7. What is the downside, if any, to providing this sort of unconditional security? What are the potential benefits?

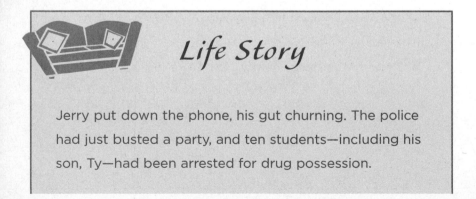

Life Story

Jerry put down the phone, his gut churning. The police had just busted a party, and ten students—including his son, Ty—had been arrested for drug possession.

Jerry had always been tough. His son had a rebellious streak, and he didn't want Ty to make the same
destructive mistakes he'd made as a teenager. Jerry had
cracked down after several recent bad grades, making
the seventeen-year-old forego several weeks of parties
and activities. And because Ty had actually snuck out
once during his grounding, Jerry told him that he would
have to drop out of the soccer team during the height
of the season. Ty had been furious, but after that he
had come home every day as required, done his homework, and brought his grades up. Believing his son had
learned his lesson, Jerry had lifted the grounding just a
few days ago—and now this.

At the station, Ty tried to explain, his face anxious:
"Dad, listen. I swear, I've never tried drugs before—
never! The guys dared me to try pot just to see what
it was like, and I refused to do any of the harder drugs,
even though they ragged on me. I know I shouldn't
have done it, and honestly I hated it. I'll never do anything like that again—"

Jerry interrupted. "This judge is a tough one—
especially about drugs—and I just heard that he wants
to send every one of you to juvenile detention for a
week just to 'teach those kids a lesson.' And I'm won-
dering whether I should let him."

Case Study Questions

1. What is Jerry's primary concern about his son? What might he expect would come from allowing the judge to send his son to juvenile detention for a week instead of fighting for a lighter sentence?

2. Now, put yourself in Ty's shoes. Based on what you've learned in this chapter, list the feelings that he may already have about his father and his approach to discipline. What new ones might be added as he waits to go before the judge?

3. Stay in Ty's shoes. What does he expect his father to say to the judge? What might the next sequence of events look like through Ty's eyes? Does he see any positives in that scenario?

4. You're still Ty. Describe the feelings he'll have if his dad stands up in the hearing and says, "He's a good kid who made a bad choice. Please don't send him to juvenile detention. Give him another consequence; I think he's already learned his lesson."

5. What are the potential benefits and drawbacks of Ty's dad approaching the situation that way? What would you do if this was your child? Explain your reasons.

6. Review "Assurance #1," starting on page 94 of *For Parents Only.* What impact might it have on Ty if his father would apply some of these principles in the months to come? What impact might it have had if he would have applied these principles in the previous months and years?

Kid Perspective: "Most of my friends' parents are too lenient, but some are too hard. Kids need to see their parents making an effort to understand them—and taking the time to talk things through."

Parent Response: During an average conflict with your child, how much time do you take to talk through the issues and understand their perspective?

> <u>Weekly Challenge:</u> (1) Every day this week, find one way to demonstrate that you want to understand your child and are trying to be a part of her world, then watch how she responds. (2) Each time you take charge this week by drawing firm boundaries or enforcing a rule, also try to say or do something that makes it clear to your child that you care about her, not just about rules. Observe her response, if any, and compare it to how she usually reacts when you exercise your authority.

Someone Once Said...

"To be in your children's memories tomorrow, you have to be in their lives today." —Anonymous

"Children need love, especially when they do not deserve it."
—Harold S. Hulbert

BRINGING IT HOME:
CONVERSATIONS WITH
YOUR CHILD ON SECURITY

Hey, Kids...

- I want to make more of an effort to show you how much I care about you and how much I want to remain connected even as you become more independent. What are one or two ways you'd like me to be more involved in your life?

- How secure do you feel about expressing yourself in this home, based on the way I usually react to you? What are some of the things I do or say that help you know that I love and support you?

- Do you ever feel like I'm not there for you when you mess up? Can you give me an example of how I could have handled something better, while still letting you experience the consequences of your actions? When you make a mistake, what would you most like to hear me say and do, even if I have to enforce discipline?

- Do you worry that you could ever do something that would make me love you less? Can you give examples of what I do to make you feel that way? What would help you believe that I'll always be here for you, no matter what?

- Do I ever make you feel as if you're not a priority in my life? Can you give me some examples?

- I'm struggling to find a balance between respecting your need for privacy and freedom and staying connected with what's really going on with you. How would you suggest I do that?

Optional: How would your child answer the survey?
- Do you think any of your friends are afraid to tell their parents what's really going on with them? Why do you suppose that is? Do you feel safe telling me what's going on in your life? What can I do to help you feel safer?
- Do your friends ever complain about their parents judging them? What do they mean when they say their mom or dad is judgmental? How does it seem to affect their relationship?

The BIG Idea

The one main idea I'm taking away from this week's discussion is...

_____

_____

_____

_____

_____

_____

_____

CAN YOU HEAR ME NOW?

*Why your teen is convinced he can't talk
to you, and how to change his mind*

Weekly Challenge Report: What are some of the
ways you showed your child that you're trying to
be a part of her world? When you found a need to
take charge, how did you assure your child that you
care more about the relationship than the rules?
What responses did you observe when you demon-
strated your love and support in these ways?

Recap

One of the biggest complaints among kids is that parents don't listen to
them. What they really mean, though, is that parents aren't listening in the
way kids need. In order to feel listened to, your child needs you to first
address his feelings about a problem before asking if he wants your help
to fix it. When parents "freak out"—showing either strong negative *or*
positive emotions—kids tend to shut down. But if you'll remain calm,

acknowledge his feelings, probe gently, and prove that you can be trusted with whatever he tells you, your child will feel safe opening up to you about the things that matter most.

"It turns out that, for our kids, listening means hearing and acknowledging what they are feeling about a problem, first and foremost." —FPO, p. 115

"I'd love to talk with my parents more. I need them, but I am afraid that they'll overreact if they really know what's going on in my heart and life." —teen quoted in FPO, p. 121

Key Questions

1. What's the most surprising thing you learned about your child from this chapter? about yourself?

2. Think about the last time your child talked to you about a problem. How long did you listen before jumping in with a solution? How did your child react to your words? If you've tried listening and affirming feelings—for example, "I can see how that would seem unfair and make you angry"—how did your kid's response differ in that situation?

3. What are your main roadblocks to listening to and acknowledging your child's feelings first? What solutions might help you overcome those?

4. Think about the last time your child accused you of not listening. Which of the translations on pages 115–23 of *For Parents Only* might get to the heart of what she really meant? What could you have done differently in that situation to prove yourself a good listener?

5. In what ways do you think your kid might perceive you to be freaking out (in a negative or even positive way) when he tells you about something he's doing or thinking? What can you do to project an air of calm and understanding?

6. If you had to guess, would your kid say you tend toward lectures or toward two-way discussions? How can you improve your communicating and listening style?

7. In a letter written to the first-century church, James—a Christian leader—wrote this: "Let every person be quick to hear, slow to speak, slow to anger; for the anger of man does not produce the righteousness that God requires" (James 1:19–20). What might this mean in practical terms for your relationship with your child?

Life Story

Kaitlyn sat quietly at the dinner table, while her siblings chattered about school. Finally, after all the other kids had put their dishes in the sink and left the kitchen, Kaitlyn's mom nudged her husband and nodded toward Kaitlyn, who still sat picking at her almost-untouched food.

Kaitlyn's dad began to wash the dishes as her mom sat down and leaned across the table. "Is something wrong, honey?" Kaitlyn shook her head, but her mom reached over and put her hand on her arm. "You're not yourself tonight, sweetheart. What's going on?"

Kaitlyn shrugged off her mother's hand, then sighed. "My soccer coach just told me I'll probably be second string all season. Again. All my friends are starting this year, except me. I'll be mostly sitting on the bench." She paused. "And Coach Jones implied, well…"

"What?"

"He implied that I'm not fast enough to be a good halfback because I'm not as trim as the other girls."

Kaitlyn's mom was furious and saw that her husband looked ready to rip the coach to shreds. She turned back to her daughter, struggling for the right words.

Case Study Questions

1. Put yourself in Kaitlyn's shoes. How might her coach's comment affect her self-image now? in the future?

2. Now, stay in Kaitlyn's shoes. Is the answer to question 1 something she thinks her parents could help with?

3. List the reasons Kaitlyn may have been reluctant to share this with her parents.

4. Stay in Kaitlyn's shoes. Why might she have shrugged off her mother's hand?

5. Based on what you've learned in this chapter, what are some responses Kaitlyn's mom and dad should avoid, and why? Describe the best way, from Kaitlyn's perspective, her parents could handle this situation, including the first words they should say.

6. You're still Kaitlyn. What's going on in her mind and heart when she hears her parents' responses?

7. What should be the next step for Kaitlyn's parents, if any?

Kid Perspective: "Sometimes parents don't listen at all. Sometimes I'm trying to tell them something, but I'm dying for them to read between the lines and figure out the real problem. I once told my parents that I was really feeling peer pressure at school, and they started coming up with all these solutions instead of pressing just a bit further and asking more questions. What I was really trying to tell them was that I was becoming bulimic. I just couldn't say it outright because I was afraid."

Parent Response: How good do you think you are at reading between the lines in your kid's statements or moods? What might help you improve your skill in addressing your child's emotions and the root issues of a problem, rather than focusing on the "fix"?

> **Weekly Challenge:** (1) Go on a "kid date" this week and see if you can really listen to your child. (You might use a Bringing It Home question to get the conversation rolling.) (2) When you feel compelled to jump in with a solution, try to resist your impulse, practice listening to and affirming his emotions, and only then ask if you can help. Notice the effect on his mood as you let him talk through his concern.

Someone Once Said...

"One important reason to stay calm is that calm parents hear more. Low-key, accepting parents are the ones whose children keep talking."
—Mary Pipher

BRINGING IT HOME: CONVERSATIONS WITH YOUR CHILD ON LISTENING

Hey, Kids...

- What are some things I do or say that make you feel like I'm really listening to you? What makes you feel like I'm not?
- Do you think I ever freak out when you tell me things? Could you give me specific examples so I understand what that looks like?
- Do you feel safe in telling me your feelings? What are some examples of things I do—or you wish I'd do—to help you feel safer?
- What's the best thing that's happening in your life right now? What's the biggest frustration you're dealing with?
- Is there anything on your mind that you've been wishing you could tell me about but thought I was too busy to really hear?

Optional: How would your child answer the survey?

- When you tell me about a problem or frustration you're dealing with, would you rather I just listen and let you talk it through, or would you like me to first offer to help?

The BIG Idea

The one main idea I'm taking away from this week's discussion is...

_____

_____

_____

_____

_____

_____

Seven

ATTITUDE ADJUSTMENT

*What mood swings reveal about
teens' secret fears, and how you
can boost their confidence*

<u>Weekly Challenge Report:</u> Did you go on a
"kid date" and talk to your child? What effect
did it have when you made an effort to affirm
his feelings?

Recap

Many of the actions and words parents perceive as attitude problems actually stem from our children's gender-specific fears and insecurities. In general terms, a boy most fears being perceived as a failure, and he most needs to feel respected. Sullenness and anger are typically signals that he's feeling inadequate, powerless, or disrespected. A girl, on the other hand, most fears being rejected, and she most needs to feel accepted and lovely, inside and out. Lippiness and sarcasm often indicate that her deepest insecurities have been triggered. By actively countering their fears and building up their confidence, we can play a key role in helping our kids grow into the engaging young men and women they most want to be.

"Giving regular affirmation, encouragement, and praise is one of the most effective ways to build confidence in our sons and create a positive cycle." —*FPO, p. 147*

"While daughters need affirmation from both parents, regular encouragement from a father has a particularly powerful, lasting impact." —*FPO, p. 161*

Key Questions

1. What surprised you most in this chapter?

2. Which of the items on the following fears-and-needs charts ring true for your child? From what you've observed, check all that apply. Then answer this question: which fear and which need do you think ranks highest for your child?

What the Guys Said	
"I most fear..."	**"I most need to feel..."**
○ failure	○ able
○ feeling inadequate	○ successful
○ being watched and found wanting	○ that people are watching and commenting on my success
○ feeling powerless	○ respected
○ appearing weak	○ accomplished
○ not being respected	○ powerful
○ not being the best at something	○ that I'm looked up to
○ no one noticing when I achieve something	○ significant

What the Girls Said	
"I most fear / am most insecure about..."	**"I most need to feel..."**
○ rejection	○ accepted
○ what people think of me	○ included
○ how I look	○ known and liked for who I really am
○ being talked about behind my back	○ special
○ not being included	○ unique
○ having people think something negative about me that isn't true	○ lovely/beautiful inside and out
○ not being known, accepted, and liked	○ that others enjoy being around me / are drawn to me
○ not being unique or valuable	○ pursued
○ being invisible	

3. Think back to the last time your kid snapped at you for seemingly no good reason...or stomped off to his room...or put on his headphones and sat sullenly alone.

   a. If you pursued the issue at the time, did your child share what was going on inside? If so, what turned out to be the reason(s)? What, if anything, surprised you about what your child was feeling, and why?

   b. If you didn't pursue it at the time (or didn't get any response!), what do you now think might have been at the root of this behavior?

4. How does your child show that his core insecurities have been triggered?

5. If you have both guys and girls at your house, what differences have you observed in how they deal with feelings of insecurity? What changes might help you better meet the unique needs of each kid?

6. How can you handle your kid's attitudes in a way that builds confidence but *doesn't* tolerate disrespect?

7. Parents of boys: As you reflect on recent interactions with your son, where might you have unintentionally communicated— either verbally or through your body language—a lack of respect for him or his abilities? What will you do differently next time you face a similar situation?

8. Parents of girls: As you think about how sensitive your daughter is to any hint of rejection, can you think of anything you've said recently that may have wounded her, *or* where you missed an opportunity to build her up when she was feeling rejected by others? If you could have a do-over, how would you rephrase your response?

Note: The case study in this chapter is focused on boys, but if desired, parents of girls can adapt it as a story of a daughter applying for a "princess" job or by exploring the chapter 6 case study on pages 52–53 in greater detail.

Life Story

Sixteen-year-old Jason bounded into the house and plopped down at the kitchen table, where his parents were drinking coffee. "Guess what?" he said. "Surprise! I just had my first job interview! I'm applying at the new Medieval Theatre in town. I think it went really well."

"No kidding!" Jason's dad said. "What did you apply for?"

"A knight!" At his parents' startled looks, Jason grinned. "You know—as in riding horses and jousting and rescuing the fair princess."

Jason's parents looked at each other, eyebrows raised. Their son loved horses, but his experience was limited to a few rides at his uncle's farm over the years and a week's vacation at a dude ranch last summer. Jason's mom finally spoke up. "But...you don't ride horses that often—"

His father interrupted. "Did they suggest that job, or did you?"

Jason's smile faded. "They had a list of jobs to choose from, and that's the one I picked, okay? I can do this! I'm very athletic, and they train you. It pays the best of all the jobs, and it'll just be on the weekends."

Jason's parents didn't know what to say. Finally, Jason's dad shrugged, "Well, good luck, Son." His mom chimed in. "Yes, and maybe you can call them back and let them know you'll be fine with working the gift shop too."

"I knew it," said Jason as he shoved back his chair. "My own parents don't believe in me. Fine. I'll just go get a McJob." Stomping off, he grunted, "Are you happy now?"

Case Study Questions

1. Why did Jason's parents have reservations about this job? What was their fear?

2. Now, put yourself in Jason's shoes. Why might he have applied for this particular job? List the possible things he wants to get out of it—both external and internal.

3. Stay in Jason's shoes. If he knows the job will be a stretch for him, what is his deepest fear? his deepest need?

4. How do you think Jason felt about his parents' responses to his news? What message did it give him? What message was he desperately hoping for?

5. How could Jason's parents have handled things differently? What would have been the downside and the upside of doing so?

Kid Perspective: "When we act certain ways when we're feeling bad, we don't want you to ask just the obvious questions or give the cliché answers. We're trying to tell you guys that we're insecure about something, and we're needing to know we're okay people you believe in. I'm sure we'll know that in college, but right now we need this assurance. Personally, I wish my folks would understand that I rant and rave at home because I can't do it anywhere else. It's not really that I'm so mad at my parents but that my parents have proven able to handle my emotions."

Parent Response: How do you handle the various emotions churning around in your kid on a day-to-day basis? How well do you distance yourself from your own emotions and fears and give your child the affirmation she really needs to conquer hers? How can you improve your handling of her unsettling emotions?

> Weekly Challenge: Observe your child this week
> to see if you notice any external signs of inner
> insecurity or fear. Rather than dealing with it
> solely as an attitude problem, try responding in
> a way that doesn't tolerate disrespect yet helps
> to boost that sagging confidence.

Someone Once Said...

"Parents need to fill a child's bucket of self-esteem so high that the rest of the world can't poke enough holes to drain it dry." —Alvin Price

"The things a man has to have are hope and confidence in himself against odds, and sometimes he needs somebody, his pal or his mother or his wife or God, to give him that confidence." —Clark Gable

"The deep cry of a little girl's heart is *am I lovely?* Every woman needs to know that she is exquisite and exotic and *chosen.*" —John Eldredge

BRINGING IT HOME:
CONVERSATIONS WITH YOUR
CHILD ON ATTITUDE

Hey, Kids...

- Do you feel that I'm generally tuned in to what's really happening inside you when you're dealing with some concern, or am I missing some signals you're trying to send about what you're struggling with? Can you give me some examples of what it looks like when you're feeling discouraged?

- When you're feeling discouraged, disrespected, angry, lonely, rejected, or insecure because of things going on in other areas of your life, what can I do to encourage you? How can I do it in a way that you find helpful instead of annoying?

- Do you feel that I respect and value you as a person? Do I ever do anything that undermines your confidence in yourself? What do I say or do that builds it up? Specific examples would help.

Optional: How would your child answer the survey?

- If you feel comfortable doing so, tell me how you'd answer the actual survey questions from this chapter (see next page). How would your answers—or those of the kids you know—compare with those of the teens who took the national survey?

Question for boys: If something happens to make you feel powerless and disrespected, how are you likely to react? (Choose all correct answers.)

○ I would be angry.

○ I would blow up.

○ I would get quiet and think it over.

○ I would be sullen and grumpy.

○ I'd stuff it and probably blow up later.

○ I'd cry.

○ I would pour out all my feelings to a friend.

○ I would compensate by trying to be powerful and respected in another area.

Question for girls: When you're mouthing off to your parents, what feelings are most likely going on inside you? (Choose all correct answers.)

○ I despise my parents.

○ I know everything, and they know nothing.

○ I'm just not feeling great about myself right now.

○ I'm feeling fearful, anxious, or defensive.

○ I'm feeling misunderstood.

○ I'm feeling unloved, unappreciated, or neglected.

○ How I'm reacting to my parents may not have as much to do with them as it does with what is going on in my life right now.

○ I'm trying to attack my parents and make them feel bad.

The BIG Idea

The one main idea I'm taking away from this week's discussion is…

_____

_____

_____

_____

_____

_____

_____

Eight

IN CASE YOU EVER WONDER...

What your child most wants to tell you

<u>Weekly Challenge Report:</u> Did you spot any signs of insecurity camouflaged as a bad attitude? How did you respond? And how did your child respond to you?

Recap

When faced with the question of what they'd most want to say today if they knew they would lose their parents tomorrow, the very same kids who earlier confessed to fighting their parents' identity and rules at every turn gave an outpouring of heartfelt responses. The kids most wanted to tell their mother and father how much they love and appreciate them... and how sorry they are for not always acting like it. Bottom line: even though it may not show right now, your child likely holds in his heart tremendous love, value, and respect for you. And one day you'll see the reward for all your efforts to connect during these turbulent, wonderful, challenging, infuriating, and highly rewarding years.

"Even though I have not acted like it all the time, I just want to let you know that I love you. Thank you for pushing me to become the best person that I could possibly be. Even though I may have felt that you were being unfair, I realize now that it was all worth it and that you did it because you love me." —teen quoted in FPO, pp. 168–69

Key Questions

1. How would you feel at hearing the above quote from a real flesh-and-blood teenager if you were this kid's parents?

2. Before you read this chapter, what did you expect that an average teenager would most want to express to a parent?

3. Do you think your children's emotional swings and words are reliable indicators of how they feel about you?

4. Were you surprised that even the kids who claim to hate their parents during a conflict will turn around and express their undying love and gratitude in this way? Why or why not?

5. Knowing that you may never hear these things under normal circumstances, how do you think your child would answer that survey question today? How does that compare with what you'd like your child to be able to say?

6. If there's a gap between what you think your child would say today and what you'd hope he would say, what steps could you take on your end to improve things?

Note: We've omitted the case study and some other features from this last chapter to give you time and opportunity to think through how you will continue to apply the *For Parents Only* findings and the personal insights you've gained from this discussion guide during the weeks and months ahead.

In addition to tackling the following questions, if you have not been doing the Bringing It Home sections, we suggest that you look back through them and pick a few questions as a starting point for some new dialogue with your kids.

Wrap-Up Questions: Preparing for the Days Ahead

1. Take another look at the chart on pages 2–3. How have your thoughts and feelings about your relationship with your child changed as you've bravely progressed through this discussion guide? What points most challenged you? What points most encouraged you?

2. Ask your child to look at the same chart and identify the areas she would most like to see you focus on. Note her answer here:

3. Based on all you've learned, what action items do *you* want
   to continue to work on in the weeks and months ahead? For
   example, what three things do you most want to do differently
   than before? *Going forward, I will:*

   a. _____

   b. _____

   c. _____

4. What other ideas do you plan to test out and experiment with
   in your parenting?

Someone Once Said...

"When I was a boy of fourteen, my father was so ignorant I could
hardly stand to have the old man around. But when I got to be twenty-
one, I was astonished at how much he had learned in seven years."
—Mark Twain

"Nothing you do for your children is ever wasted. They seem not to
notice us, hovering, averting our eyes, and they seldom offer thanks,
but what we do for them is never wasted." —Garrison Keillor

"To understand your parents' love you must raise children yourself."
—Chinese proverb

BRINGING IT HOME: CONVERSATIONS ABOUT WHAT YOUR CHILD REALLY WANTS YOU TO KNOW

Hey, Kids...

I've been working pretty hard the past few weeks to better understand what you're dealing with. But that said…

- Based on all the things we've discussed over the last few weeks, what do you most appreciate and think I'm now doing well? Or at least, what I am doing better?

- What would you still most like to see change and improve in our relationship going forward? How can I help make that happen? What might you do to help make that happen?

- Everybody has blind spots—faults we just can't see in ourselves. As kindly as possible, will you tell me about an important blind spot that I may still have as it relates to parenting you? How would you suggest I deal with that issue?

- If you're willing to share, I'd be really interested to hear how you'd answer the final survey question. If you prefer, you could write your answer down. Here's the question: "We want you to imagine something very difficult. If you were to somehow find out that your parents were going to die tomorrow, what would you most want to tell them today?"

- Let me tell you what I've learned about you that I didn't get before and something I really want to say about how I feel about you…

The BIG Idea

The one main idea I'm taking away from this week's discussion—and what I most want to apply in the weeks and months to come—is...

A Final Note
from the Authors

Thank you for joining us on this journey inside the head of your kid. We know the path may have been challenging, scary, and exhilarating in turn. But above all, we hope that immersing yourself in the mind and heart of your child has proven helpful to you in ways that will bear good fruit for a lifetime—and beyond.

Blessings to you as you continue your journey,

Shaunti & Lisa